the Well

New and Selected Poems

For

Leonard McDermid
with every good wish
on your National
Poetry Award.
I hope you can draw
something playful
from this Well.

John Liddy
Madrid
2010

Dedication

To the memory of
Pamela O'Malley de Crist.

John Liddy

the Well
New and Selected Poems

Preface
Desmond O'Grady

Introduction
Patrick Galvin

A WHITE HOUSE POETRY BOOK

Revival Press
Limerick - Ireland

First published in 2007 by
Revival Press
Moravia, Glenmore Avenue,
Roxboro Road,
Limerick, Ireland

www.revivalpress.ie

In association with
The WhiteHousePoets.

www.limerick.com/whitehousepoets

Designed and set by Alphaset, Limerick, Ireland
Printed by GraphyCems, Spain.
Cover Image: 'Cows Come Home' (1989) John Shinnors
Limerick City Gallery of Art. Courtesy of the artist.
Author photograph John Minihan

Project Editor Dominic Taylor

ISBN 978-0-9554722-0-6

A CIP catalogue record for this book is available from
The British Library

Revival Press acknowledges the assistance of
The Arts Council, Ireland
and Limerick.com

Acknowledgements

Previously published new poems in this collection first appeared
in Agenda; Cuadernos del Matemático; Limerick Trilogy
(a choreography by Michael Klien); Microphone On; Southword;
The Stony Thursday Book; YearBook, Madrid Young Learners;
Revival.

All other poems appeared in *Boundaries* (Janehunt Publications,
Limerick, 1974*), The Angling Cot* (Beaver Row Press, Dublin,
1991), *Song of the Empty Cage* (Lapwing Publications, Belfast,
1997), *Wine and Hope/Vino y Esperanza* (Archione Editorial,
Madrid, 1999), *Cast-A-Net/Almadraba* (Archione Editorial,
Madrid, 2003).

Thanks to Desmond O'Grady for his Preface, Patrick Galvin
for his Introduction, John Shinnors for his cover image and
John Minihan for author photograph.

Special Thanks to Frank McCourt, Knute Skinner and
Micheál Fanning for support and encouragement and to Bertha
McCullagh and Liam Liddy for proof-reading and helpful advice.

Preface

This collection of poems by John Liddy is his sixth published book. In it he has made a selection from the poems in his five previous books and has added a group of new poems up to 2007.

The book creates a map of his life where his poems were and are inspired. John Liddy is one of those rare people who motivated by his interest in literature was given a vocation to write an account of his own experiences and to become a poet. In his early days, to enrich his life experience, he left Ireland to work and study abroad. His landscapes move from the Ireland of his youth to the America of his adult years and finally his return to Europe and family life in Spain.

Liddy's poems reflect the places he has lived in, the people he met and the paraphernalia of places, people and daily life. At the same time his other writing-hand translates poems into English from languages he knows such as Irish and Spanish. That creative discipline is also reflected in his poems. He lives a full life. This selected and new poems halo over his vocation as a poet and make the book a Portrait of the Poet in 2006 as an Irish European. As such he is an excellent example to all students and readers of literature who themselves aspire to write.

Desmond O Grady

Introduction

With the launch of the literary review 'The Stony Thursday Book' in the mid seventies, John Liddy and Jim Burke greatly improved the literary landscape for those of us who inhabit it. Their freshness, enthusiasm and sheer appreciation of language and craft signalled that a contributing poet's work was in the hands of someone who sought to enrich the existence of writers and their readers. The one serious downside of this operation was that John Liddy's time was dedicated more to the promotion of poetry than to its creation. However, with distance and time, that has been gracefully rectified with a fairly constant output from him since 1991.

One senses that the earth's magnetic pull had destined John to move to Madrid in his quest for poetic fulfilment. Once transposed, rather than transplanted to Spain, his many years there of working in a library and translating classic works from the original Irish and Spanish, enriched his poetic talents he so strikingly revealed in 'Boundaries' in 1974. He developed his craft in tandem with his language skills and his universal concerns remain constant. He is among the few Irish poets who write works of an obvious romantic or lyrical nature but do not shrink from the harsher realities that life often throws up. 'Remembering Mr. Toppin', 'Emmet Dalton', 'The Absent', 'Fallen Leaves' and 'Sarsfield's Children' are examples of these latter works whilst his more romantic nature is expressed through the near-perfect lyrical poems 'Nocturne' 'Miracle', 'A Letter for Pilar' and chasing the Pigeons', poems that compose themselves effortlessly.

Most importantly, whether he is writing poems of recollection, social realism, politics, or nature, John Liddy has the ability to use language which hits the poetic 'g spot' more often than not. It awakens in us emotional, visual and intellectual responses as well as resolving or satisfying our deep need or desire for cultural expression.

Signs and portents, pregnant earth and how we dance on her - or destroy her- are never far from our thoughts when we read the poetry of this man from Munster. He merges his talents as editor, translator and poet in 'Song of The Empty Cage' to connect us with the earth, history, culture, country and each other; both as poets and as readers.

When re-reading 'The Angling Cot' and the 'Cast-A-Net' poems I am once again reassured of the strength of their rhythms, the power of their images, the sureness of their language and the writer's ability to reflect a reality or an aspiration through poetry. For me as a poet there are two questions I ask of any poem: Is it worth writing? If I haven't written it would I like to have written it? For many poems in this current collection the answer is a resounding Yes.

Patrick Galvin

CONTENTS

New Poems
The Well (2007)

Selected Poems

Cast-A-Net (2003)

Wine and Hope (1999)

New Poems

the Well

(2007)

"We who drink from the well must
never forget those who dug it".

From the Irish.

TAKING STOCK
to Jim

Travellers, there is no path, paths are made by walking.

1.
With half the Appian Way
behind us, let me conduct
some honest inventory,
measure what is still intact.

My sons are quiffing-up
for dance floors barred to me;
their mother readies her cinema
self to leave me to my reality.

I watch in awe how life slips
through my fingers, subtle
as needles knitting new stories;
know why the inevitable

Is not worth the effort of futile
contemplation, why we endure
the weight on thin shoulders;
love on despite erosion.

2.
Allow me to fix on the personal,
the art in what is uniquely found
because of casual destiny,
simple scenes but universal.

That first taste of deception –
footing the miserable road home
out of Dublin after Van's
walk-off and we still listening.

Or that bicycle tour of the West,
noted but lost, still haunting
like Connemara fields; our tent
a classroom of free-talk

Without teachers amidst the Aran
schoolhouse ruin, the stroll back
from MacPhadraig's public house
after a night of music and *craic*

As Gaeilge, between the famine
dead lit by a touchable moon.
Or those abandoned boots beside
a sparse tree in Spiddal.

3
Other matters demand attention
But we choose what to ignore:
the private cravings of the heart,
A lame excuse for war.

No. I will leave them aside
to concentrate on bare essentials.
Such stock makes truth of our lives,
not headlined but what survives.

I have paced enough of the house
like a dog in search of its spot
to bury its bone. It is time to sit
and write this down.

TRIVIAL PURSUIT

I close the door
on domestic squabble
between my sons
and their mother.

My world of concerns
with friendly fire
and collateral damage
is too fragile

To allow such trivia
erode the flow of line,
invade my thought,
bombard my syllable.

Later I notice a calm
in the living room,
forgotten actions,
no casualties.

ANOTHER ELEVENTH IN THE LIBRARY
for my students

Today I went to work
with the weight of death and mutilation
in my shoulder bag; incalculable loss
like sinking stones in my pockets,
the pens and pencils rattling
to the sound of severed bones
across the floor of a bombed train,
the books and papers
smeared with destiny's blood
stopped in its tracks.

Opening the library door
I saw everything in its place
except myself –
the tidied shelves and shiny plants,
hoovered carpet and clean glass-reflection.
But my chair was no longer mine
beside a desk that pined
for somebody else,
the in-tray for the reach
of another hand.

Then duty slowly called
me to my station
in the face of a child
who needed a book
about animals
in danger of extinction.

FATHER'S DAY

My sons ask about the validity of war.
I answer killing is wrong. What you see
on television is from a privileged position.
No civilian suffering and might is right.

But in young minds thoughts collide.
Is it wrong to kill the fatted calf for shoe,
the mad bull for fun, the mink for fur,
the crocodile for wallet, the whale for oil,
the tree for paper, the plant for medicine,
the insect for curiosity, the spider's web?

In the name of God and official uniform,
disobedient enemies, state terrorists,
the innocent in Omagh or Oklahoma,
the goose that lays the golden egg,
words that have lost their meaning,
dying languages, freedom's thoughts?

Yes, I answer, it is wrong to kill,
despite the approval of public opinion.

THE EMPTY EMBRACE

Everybody agreed.
Instead of photographs
a commissioned artist
to record the deed.

A sculptor to sculpt
the destruction *in situ*,
make art from metal
scraps for all to see.

The hand sought
to catch the repentant
mood of Armalites
in sackcloth

Dumb expressions
on mortar bombs,
trickles of rust oozing
from snipers' rifles.

At the unveiling,
nobody noticed
that the arms
were missing.

THE WELL

When I gazed into the well and saw the horror,
not even the minor miracles of Borges
could lift my head to face the one-legged man
with a hand out for a coin on my street corner,
or contemplate light on leaves in the Sorolla
garden before daily routine began in a library
born from a shoebox and grown to half blossom.

Everyday magic was reduced to banality,
as though witnessing a parade of Pavlov's dogs,
prophecies of Pound's botched civilisation,
the New Order clamouring for more war
with God and Alá in the cockpit guided by remote
experts who dropped bombs before breakfast
with one eye on the slush movie.

Perhaps I should have stayed in bed? Tortured
myself with images from any rat infested cell,
or simply run my finger over a small town
mid-western windowsill to reveal raw vengeance.
Or planned for shelters under bloodied skies -
innumerable maimed to heal, innumerable dead
to bury, the stone's thud in the muddied well.

What can I say for my wish to come true?
That old Europe is not a sick animal dying
by the roadside with green juice oozing
from its mouth, gasping for its last breath
before the hero of the hour comes blazing
to the rescue with friendly fire.

That I have wiped the yawn from my boots
after trampling through fields of earth's heaven,
returned to my street with the clear well
of my being sated by the taste of spring water
to quench the thirst for destruction,
complete the library to pass on, face the one-
legged man, never again to doubt the minor
miracle, the end of knowledge with the death
of every old African, the well dug by ancestral
sweat for me to drink from, the cave's echo
at my back resounding ...

THE ABSENT

On this summer morning I sit
With the sound of water at my back
And watch the crowds visit.

There is the temptation to criticise
The woman on her mobile arranging
To meet at the Palacio de Cristal,

The mother reprimanding her son,
Owners of barking dogs or my own
Inadequacy on that eleventh of March

When I tried to answer questions
From my sons as the breakfast radio
Announced details of the carnage.

I walk home through the city noise,
Knowing there is enough silence
And sorrow present all year round

In this commemorative coniferous
Forest of the absent, to last one
Hundred and ninety one lifetimes.

GONE

There he was –
gone from the bed
he slept in,
a favourite chair
shaped by him
like a snipe's lair
after flight.

Nothing left
but lingering scent
of memory,
tepid feel
of personality,
images of being
never to spring alive,
fill the space
he once occupied.

THE PETER PAN DIARY 1978
i.m. Mary Keyes

This was the year you found and lost God
between mood swings and musical nights
in country pubs, bad days in the hospital.

When friends called with reservoirs of chat
to ease your angst, fill their own vacuums
with charitable attempts at comforting.

The occasional warmth of a pillowed arm
not enough to safeguard you in sleep
or seduce you onto the road of recovery.

We were too busy with youth to notice
the serious glare in your eye, the failure
of Dr. O'Connell's benevolent touch.

That time, so long ago, my name frozen
on the page of the last entry, the stones
of your words in my pockets, as I walk

Each year to decipher the river, to listen
for the notes of your whistle, a tune played
in Murroe, laughter in the laps of water.

FALLEN LEAVES

I used to think they were all
Put back on the trees each spring
By the keepers of parks and glens.

Raised from soggy graves to dazzle
And dance in sunshine and wind,
Their sacred hearts a redemption

Of souls, cracked spines healed,
Proof of miraculous resurrection.
But such thoughts dwindled

As I heard of friends trampled on.
No nimble Cuchulainn or light-
Footed deer to guide and shelter

Them in groves through winter,
Bellow their hearts to glow
Like maples in summer.

Frail as leaves they fell,
Never to recover.

HARRI
for Pomma

First I noticed the smile,
His hallmark. Then the glinting eye
And a face full of intelligence.

When he spoke words sprang
From wells dug beyond his years,
Delivered with exactitude.

He was an apparition in troubled
Times, a soothsayer for the tormented,
Bending the tarot's secret sign

To ease the victim's burden.
In Limerick and Madrid
Our friendship was sealed

Until personal journeys diverged.
You dear Harri to the fruits of the soil
In a town too small for your magic.

Me to carry on towards what I am.
Though time erodes memory
I see you urging us eternally.

FURTHER THOUGHTS

to Patrick Finnan

I am now the one grappling with words
On reading your *Thought at Donaghmore.*
A tribute to that ancient burial ground,
The seedbed of my father and mother.

In every line and rain-swept syllable
The notes of friendship sounding clear
To me in the Sierra de Madrid where I walk,
Their wind-music whispering to me here

Vivid as the poem penned by your hand
In the familiar shade of cypress and palm,
The perfume of childhood's hawthorn blossom
Real as the tomb's finite surname.

NOCTURNE

I have heard again the faint
Phantom notes floating in
From the patio to where I work.

Gathering momentum, fluidity,
Until the whole piece plays out
With command and delicacy,

The touch of keys dissolving
Around me, stirring a memory.
Woken as a child by the sound

Of my father's lonesome piano,
I would creep in to sit near him
On the floor without a word,

Mesmerised by his magic,
Sensitive to a private sadness,
Until the lid closed with a sigh

And I slept consoled by music
In my dreams and by images
I would one day compose.

CONVERSATIONS WITH PLAQUES

In my stride along the same route
Home from work all year round,
I use the distance to unwind,
Think myself into moods to tackle
Ideas impatient for completion.

When least expected I am joined
For a block or two by Hernández
Who slows me to a snail's pace
More suited to shepherds with time
To kill or poets who have found

Their rhythm. I learn much from him
As we walk along Conde De Peñalver
Touching on Cradlesongs of the Onion
Or the three hurts: life, love, death.
Then he is gone, back to his prison

Wall, now an old womens' home.
But I am not alone for long. Quiet
As a butterfly Lorca slips in. He talks
About his childhood in Granada,
How he is fearful of departure

And why he must run naked again
In the meadow, show the mobs
What they are made of, try and stop
The haemorrhage with verse.
Before I reach my front door

He is readying to leave his rooms
On Alcála, prepare his farewells.
Later, as I sit at my table and think
About the company I keep,
I know exactly what I must do.

A MOMENT OUTSIDE THE SELF

Project into a future landscape
Where pecking crows claim the seed,
Defy robotic waving of arms
As high-flying birds the sky.

And if there is still such a thing
As a country walk let your shadow
Take its own direction, return
With the harvest in your eye.

By then scarecrow will have gone
To the rag and bone shop.
So it is your responsibility to note
Minute detail, seasonal subtleties.

Observe carefully the famished child
Dying on his dead mother's breast,
While children hide and seek amidst
The high stalks of the wheat field.

If extra sensory you may even
Stop the bullet from finding home,
Quell the order before it is given
To drop the bomb.

Perhaps you might prevent a fall.
See something simply beautiful –
A child tying her grandfather's
Lace and you all agog.

IN THE LIBRARY OF THE MIND

There will always be streets full of hope.
Public places held together by strings of goodwill.
Handsome men and women out for evening strolls,
The day's chores done, peace in dreams,
The echo of bird song in sleep.

Children will climb into big books
Where ferocious animals protect them at night,
The drip of evergreen forests slake their thirst
And each page a tactile discovery of worlds,
Escape mechanisms, pleasure in curiosity.

But sometimes doors to knowledge are shut,
Information restricted, data manipulated.
Truth lives in solitary confinement,
Memory betrays thought and effort
Is pain, blank, pointless.

We become other shades of the self,
Grow forgetful; surrender to change,
The wind's whim, the circle's imprisonment;
Survive somewhere between blindness
At birth and old age, the first and last spoonful.

For the fortunate who have found plenty
In bare necessity and see beyond walls,
Love glows in dark corners, shines eternally.
What is made is reaped between the bloom
And death of seeds, a stone's ripple.

A SORIAN VILLAGE IN AUTUMN

From the ring road it looks like a painter's
study of how roof and wall can merge
with the land in a confluence of russet reds.

Only animal sounds and shimmering poplars
in the morning light whisper of life and death
within the frame. The sign proclaims a name

But nothing human stirs as we advance –
smoke from a conical chimney, wood piles,
frosted cow dung and a cat skulking home

From a party convey the impression time
Stopped long ago in this isolated village.
I could be walking in the footsteps of Celt-

Iberians, Romans, Muslims... or spied on
by the guardians of the canyons, amongst
the murmuring of a poet's river that hums

Of concord in the warm kitchens of bone-
chilled nights with people who out-sing
the onslaught of winter as if it were their last.

MUD

In the heat of the contest on the strand,
Spear and Sword discarded their *luminis*
For the thieving tide to make the river
Cloakful. Hence the name *Luimenach.*

As children we saw the rags of warrior-
Ghosts cling to reeds outside our reach,
Trodden and worn to threads by history's
Hardened lessons in the muck of war.

I was a boy defying the mechanical digger
That bulled the bare marsh for housing
On *Inis Sibhtonn*, my world of squelch
And semiliquidity made my hands splinter

With the winter's awe of a one-syllabled
Word - a child's earthy toy - cannon balls
Drying in the sun, a blacksmith's lance
For poking fun at the enemy anthill.

I grew up with larks near the coalyards,
Crushers guarding the castle gates, slingers
And daubed walls, the landslide of islands
Bound for freedom and the open seas -

A futile dash. The opaqueness of it all.
But I can still feel the presence of *láib*
In the prosperous settlements by the river,
Salute the return to origins in peacetime.

GLISSADES

*

An old man
dozes the afternoon away
in the quiet of a small hotel.
Breath that once calmed
turbulent waters
filled youth's sail.

He is the plight of the elderly
whose bell nobody rings.
When he dreams of company
he once knew he knows
the world has deceived.

*

She was the protest
outside Embassies
with hands made for placards.
The rewards for her struggle
what she gave to others.

*

Somebody once said
'you can cut down all the flowers
but cannot stop the spring'
I say you can kill for money
and not have the price of a coffin.

*

Two shells trap the sea notes in his head,
lap his private shore to hum along the way,
the music of fish and coral in memory,
a stranger to the place he once knew.

He is a plough without a field
to furrow because he left
his heart in Conor Pass.

*

We are echoes of our own departures,
trapped in locked wells nobody drinks from
or will taste again on summer tongues.

We are the shift from script to print.
Between Black Death and Colón
the Renaissance gave birth
to a slobbering of snow
in the sun's thaw.

*

The things shepherds have seen
do not surprise.
When the world sleeps there is always
one daisy awake, a fallen star to guide them
along the path through the bog.

*

A woman at the late night bar sings the blues
while another on her knees scrubs the floor.
Glissades for the passing audience
to find their own steps home.

OLD FLAMES

When they met again a thought
entered the space between them.
Both surprised that such distance
could still claim rights once enjoyed
in each other's company.

Perhaps time after all is a friend,
nudging us to be true and not allow
circumstance disturb what two people
stumble on together in spite of themselves
and the ever so slow burnout.

A BEEHIVE HUT
for María and Paul on their wedding

Unlike Diarmuid and Gráinne
Who loved tirelessly on the run
Without a place to call their own,
You can now from this day on
Choose together with care each stone
To corbel the strata's centre,
Craft each stratum's tilt
To shed the rains in winter,
Deflect the winds of sudden storm.

From this day on you can set
Your capstone at the top to let
Difficulties fly out, sunshine in,
Construct an echo chamber of song
With banks and fosses to prevent
Raids on love's private store,
Guard the harvest from two lands.
Your heart's haven like a journey's
Embrace in a familiar harbour.

VISITING IRELAND
with my father-in-law, Manuel Gutierrez

On reaching Heuston Station
you praised The Galway Hooker
for ambience and quality of drink,
but voiced a sour note boarding
the train for Cork - dirt outside
the clean interior.

Was this an omen for how
the journey would be? Finding fault
at any opportunity, sprinkling
the experience with *andaluzadas*,
Cadiz's pride blinding the view
with Europe's first street light?

But as you gazed out the window
hay rolled silently in the mind,
drizzled field animals fed
from your hand and wild flowers
vied with a pallet of greens
for the praise-worthy comment.

That eye for exquisite detail
sharpened my own and kept me
focused on local knowledge
regarding creameries and crops,
rivers and farms and how it all
once fitted into the community.

I could have been with my father
travelling the hungry mile
through one-stop towns
for the sale of a dozen whiskey,
silence and talk strengthening
the bonds we were building.

Those same eyes found their true
cast on reaching the sea,
your element and home, with scales
on your boots, familiar memory
of Mercamadrid, boats
in the harbour at the ready.

In the midst of things new
and wonderful I saw a young man
talking fish in Castletownbere
or rising at five in Union Hall
to meet the catch off the trawler
and send it to a family of nine.

But what of the scenery on the road
to Dingle? Each bend a revelation
greeted with the exclamation
¡Qué barbaridad! Colourful villages
by the Atlantic's pull and call
at your heart's abode.

If only you could have it all
over again you said without words
on the return leg from Killarney,
bright eyes lost in reflection,
contemplating Milagros in Robledo,
unpacking first impressions.

A LETTER TO PILAR

Have I told you lately how much I love you
Van Morrison

This letter I never wrote but should have.
So now is the right moment to pen the patient
Page with a few words of homage.

The day you walked into the core of my being
I knew then why I had come to your Spain,
But worried about losing my Irish vocation.

Two beautiful poems later (our boys) I rethought
My obsession, worked alone in the knowledge
That you were always in me, the poem I sought.

Over the years I have watched your vigour
For friendship enrich those around you,
Comfort them with smiles and good nature

And when loss or rejection bruises me
The healing powers of those gifts as steadfast
And gentle as your inimitable philosophy.

So if I have been selfishly silent for some time
Know today, my love, that these words are poor
Substitutes for the love within you that is mine.

WHEN THE PAINTERS AND THE POETS VISIT

Like out-of-season birds they fly off the canvas
Or the page because the impulse is strong
To walk outside the margins for a change.

They might bring gifts of local ornament,
A half dozen duck eggs from the village
Or some notion as to why they are here.

Over slow breakfast talk is of fellow travellers
Who are on sabbaticals elsewhere or rooted
In the search to interpret the daily familiar.

There is seldom any obtrusive criticism.
We slide between self-exile in the metropolis,
What we have in common: zero temperatures

And the evening walk to and from the local bar
After a day's slog with magpies large as eagles,
Space where you thought there was none,

Precise punctuation, language outside arm's reach.
When they have gone I confirm by example
Their absence, breathe in the odour of friendship,

The means to carry on. Each to our own work
Within the frame. Like returned migrants
Completing our part of the bargain.

BIRTHDAY'S CANDLE
for Desmond O' Grady

In the flame's flicker
'The burden of the past
And the creative imagination',
The chord's first soundings

Tightening like the sinews
Of the solitary hero ordained
To wander the labyrinth
Fields of myth and legend,

Worship at the feet of Gaul.
Return as the insular Celt
With tracings of western
Civilisation to complete

The Sura's vexing puzzle
From your table in Kinsale –
Where you today may cast
An urgent eye at scattered

Mounds of work like beehives
Waiting to be honeyed into
Books, until there is little left
For the paperweight to hold

But fulfilment in the sigh.
Your life's purpose released,
To burn with your inheritance –
A teacher's and a poet's legacy.

TIG
for Jimmy Clancy

For the small boy the game
was all about coping under cover
with the monotony of time,
in the company of rancid smells,
close-ups of minuscule detail.

Night after night he moved
like a twig in a bush, an insect
beneath flattened grass, a fox
that held his nerve in the height
of the chase to crawl under
the chaser's nose and release
his captive friends; to bask
in the euphoria of summer's
shoulder round the darkening
fields they played in as children;
to sleep with the unanimous
applause of the undergrowth
in a world of fearful jailers
who waited for certain defeat,
ignorant of their shortcomings.

Now the chaser and the chased
touch home in different dens,
applying what each learned
in the game of tig, as equals.

SEEING THE LIGHT
for GL

He was a sinister shadow at Murphy's corner,
a fearful figure for stray dogs who skulked
from his boot, or neighbourhood children
who clutched their mother's milk money.

Tired of playing Dick Turpin with small fry
he ascended the rungs of lawlessness –
a hero on gull who first made his name
in Guard Dennihey's notebook, he swaggered

On to greater feats until Cupid cleared a space
in her haggard for a love too difficult to tend.
The years passed with a son the fountain stone
in the centre of his world, so he weeded

For his sake to find the light, kindle the cold
years of childhood. Now winter's warmed
by company in the local - their friendship
his son's inheritance, a clean slate his legacy.

ON THE NAIL
for Ger Touhy

That drive to Dublin
through a criminal fog
with Hogan's load.
The snail's pace of the truck
defying death's tunnel.
Your persistent story
about the eyes of the black dog.
At last the Port lights
guiding us to the warehouse door
where an old man gloved
in poverty's mittens
proffered a swallow-tailed coat
for a pittance.

After a night's pampering
in Fitzwilliam Square,
we filled the return leg
with raucous laughter
about the lightness of our load
and how I would look
decked out at the Art School Ball.
On reaching Limerick's High Street
emptiness greeted my smile,
for the coat had flown
back to its six-inch nail.

UNSUNG

Not you, condemned like some to a life
Incapable of love or kind act.
Those brutalised children of the New State,
Their unbearable secret shaming
Them into silence and an early grave.

You, who survived through icy strength of will
And a beautiful intellect that kept faith in one
Who showed you how to make the city's type-
Writers hum for its young men and women
In a classroom orchestrated with precision.

There, amidst the clanking of the Royals
You confiscated my early scribbling
And saw enough in them for publication.
Since then I have seen how you gave
Without asking for anything in return –

The quiet way you helped to place a farmer's
Daughter in local business or answered
The traveller's knock with a parcel of clothes.
Perhaps someday your adopted city
Will sing of what you have done.

MEMORY
for Lillian

It happens before your eyes.
Unconnected thoughts over lunch
like sudden swerves down sideroads,
then a dignified return to polite
conversation at the table.

You suspect a touch of amnesia
for not remembering your name.
And you begin to show concern
over the phone call in August
to enquire about St Patrick's
invitation to the Embassy.

But what about the details?
Recalling the 30's like yesterday,
when her brother carried her
on his bare back across the estuary
of the incoming tide, near the ruined
castle and the golf course.

You hope for recovery,
some magic to restore lucidity,
a defiant act of rebellion
that stops the erosion.

Like strangers in a waiting room
you watch the retreat into deeper
childhood, pure as new life.
All that goodness for you
to recall while you can.

FAIL BETTER
after Beckett

Every so often
a tight rope unravels.
No net to break
the fall.

A juggler's knife
escapes the hand
to find the point
of existence.

Gravity pulls
at private pain,
proffers poison
to ease the burden

Until the crawl
out of oblivion
makes us wiser
to the world's

Contradiction.
Our own unique,
exiguous place
in the chaos.

RHUBARB
for Alan Shelley

We imagined gardens of juicy stalks,
herbaceous plants cut when young
as substitutes for fruit, their purgative

Powers cleansing us; smells of childhood's
kitchen like ingredients in our conversation –
India, Turkey, Old French perhaps?

Its barbarous taste leading us from the Volga
across war-torn Europe to nuclear uncertainty
in a world that has not learned the simplicity

Of talk in a bar where two men discuss a word,
savour history as equals and dream of lifting
a slice of common goodness to their mouths.

REVENGE

Come summer's tide we will return
to steal the catch out of his mouth

Tumble him hard on craggy rock,
watch him crawl to an empty boat.

With vengeful eyes we will burn holes
in the planks, curse him to the coldest

Depths and toss his carcass onto dry land
as a sign to others who might be tempted.

For his cruelty knew no bounds when he
slaughtered our kind on Beginish Island,

Stained sheep's grazing with our blood
as a warning to others to keep out,

Bludgeoned us out of greed for gnawing
at nets and pots in the ancestral Sound.

A VIEW FROM SIBEL HEAD
for Mairín Feiritéir

Advised to keep out, I urged
my family on towards the top,
in summer rain across fields
draped like green tablecloths
over the end of old Europe

Until we found our spot and sat
to picnic close to heaven under
a sudden sun; to contemplate
the silent crawl of trawlers
like ants on liquid crystal,

The raucous racket of herring-
gulls suppering their young,
while beyond the horizon
a new empire flexed its muscle
at the helm of a rudderless world.

I could sense the electricity
of imagination soaring about
The Three Sisters like frozen
waves along the line of landscape,
memorials to the slaughter

At Smerwick, near the scattered
ruins of the poet's castle,
its stones lodged in the softness
of fertile grass, charged
with history's legacies:

The calm after battle, a peace
found in graveyards,
the victor's whim outlived
by that Norman-Irish gentleman
Piarais Feiritéir, master

Of classical Irish metre,
supplier of hunting hawks
(coaxed out of Brandon's mists)
to the FitzGeralds's of Desmond
for whom he held the Blaskets.

And there off Clogher, a vision
of a young woman out of her
depth on White Beach, as later
an admirer would be in Dublin's
Insurrection, or the last Islander

To leave forever to look back
as I looked on Wine Strand
at Dún an Óir, where Spanish
blood was spilt in vain and all
around us the tranquillity of bog;

The poet *stretched out in it here.*
I will return alone in winter
to feel the full rage of its beauty,
the barbed wire of its wind,
knowing I have been warned.

Selected Poems

Cast-A-Net

(2003)

SPOONING

for Euwan Willmott
Whom friends remember with affection

'Un arall os gwelwch yn dda' is the order of the night
As we 'deoch an doris' to the next bric-a-brac bar
Along the hymn-singing prom of Aberystwyth,
Round Bae Ceredigion and down the river
Shannon to Limerick in Madrid.

We recognise the Celt in each other's eye,
The meeting of histories in an Irish monk's book
Evading invasion in Llanbadarn church,
The leader who is also a bridge
In The Gododdin.

And what of those carved gifts of legend
In the modern design of our lives?
Those links between Bevan and Kemmy,
Song and valley, rugby and accent; lovespoons
Carried deep in clustered pockets:

The wheel, the leaves, the ball in a cage,
A single heart sent out in messages of pipe smoke
Above the talk of language and politics –
Before you parted for your bed half-made in Spain
With 'buenos noches', 'oiche mhaith', 'nos da'.

CHASING THE PIGEONS
for Marcus and Seán

I marvelled at you in springtime.
Tirelessly racing across hazardous
Cobbles to plunge into the wrought
Of an old lady's mound of crumbs,
Her annoyance banished to another
Bench where she continued to feed
Before the Plaza erupted again.

But you were only after the white one,
The one you wanted to touch
And dream of when sleep brought
That bird of peace within arm's reach.
What was it the old lady chased
When young and could not catch?
May her crumbs nourish my children,
May they grasp it in their lifetime.

MIRACLE

Suddenly happiness was everywhere.
People at peace and minor problems
Settled with a handshake or a kiss.

Nobody died of hunger, nobody was poor.

There was a noticeable improvement
In the weather, seasons defined themselves,
Cracked riverbeds healed, animals returned
From extinction, the air smelled of jasmine,
Humanity heard itself for the first time,
Listened with complete understanding.

Language knew no boundaries.

Spacecrafts stopped visiting and Gods
Decided to retreat because Earth
At last was behaving as planned,
No longer needing a helping hand.

THE PIGGERY
for Tommy

There was something of Munch's painting
In the squeal at feed-time, a deafening insistence.
The smell forever to lodge under the nostrils
Like fear in Nessa's spaniel-eyes when taking fright,
Jumped the wall, swam the width of the pit

Into the safety of my slurried arms.
It was my first real vision of the souls
In Purgatory, the damned in Hell, the true
Meaning of labour, sweat of survival,
And why the woman in the farmhouse kitchen

Reminded me of the loudest silence of all.
I learned much in that factory of snort and grunt,
Sow and boar; how he rode her from behind
Until exhaustion buckled them both,
Why the gaffer sometimes escaped to the town's

Shipless embrace of fish-eyed riverside company.
This then was my schooling in the raw world
Of man and beast, and the gravel pathway I spread
Now echoes with the crunch of other boots,
But the scream of what art is prevails.

SARSFIELD'S CHILDREN

The poor have no memory
For the sunshine of miserable times,
Picnics of hungry afternoons,
Holidays by the sea, with a view
From the tenement room of mackerel
Leaping in the laneways,
First love dancing on shiny floors
In Augustinian halls.

But what is never forgotten
Is the articulated feeling
That history bequeated the crumb,
Etched its social sting on innocent children
To house their non-existent futures
Among the cannonballed ruins
And slums of devastation.

The poor have no memory
For the humiliation of outdoor toilets,
The smell of damp clothing,
The itch of shaven heads.
Posterity is a cleansing that perfumes
The nostrils, creates a more
Frightening impoverishment.

But should you mention this
Keep it Dickensian -
You never know what toes
You might be standing on.

GER BRINN DIES IN AUSTRALIA

The news was as sudden as your heart
Stopping on a street in Melbourne.
Strangely alive again like the school-pal
We haven't seen for years. As though
It were yesterday's summer when you found
The short-cut home from the fourth boreen,
A pioneer of new gaps in the ditch,
An inkling of what was to come –
Growing away into first love
Beside the dazzling waters of Corbally,
The shame of not making a living
In the shell-shocked Limerick of the 70's.

It cannot have been Mitchell's Journal
Or letters home to Dromoland from Smith O'Brien
That set you flying to a better life among
The ghosts of United Irishmen and women.
Unlike them you were free to roam
And try your hand at carpentry.
What monuments to your family's trade
Stand today in the suburbs and living rooms,
The shops and offices of the street
Where you perhaps for a fleeting moment
Imagined family and boyhood friends
Gathered on Doolin pier for a last farewell,
The scattered ashes struggling to return.

O WINGED BIRD
i.m. Michael Hartnett

Our fathers knew each other in the music of hurling,
As we did in poems and songs, and though the years
Fill our lives with empty meeting places, I treasure
Your line 'Bóthar an fhile gan chloch mhíle air'.

There was no poetry in my milestones then, you said,
The people of Clonard and Ballymurphy would sort it out.
But I wrote my Southern Comfort in hindsight, to begin
The search for Starkie's gypsy ballads in post-Lorca Spain.

Going home to Heaney's fish-smelling balcony I found
A swallow dropped in from under the crucifying sun,
A wren handkerchiefed outside, wrapped in a blanket
From a convent bed in Santa Teresa's Encarnación.

Over dinner you let slip a jar of beetroot and for years
The stubborn stain on the tiles spoke to me of hedge birds
Claiming the ditch in spring, Templeglantine memory
Of children chasing a pig round the hillside garden.

Much of what you trawled from your travels sparkled
Afresh on the page. The day your grandmother died
During the Moroccan Madrid fling, Ó Bruadair's tortured
Tribe, the death of a GaeltEacht in Moonagay, love and exile

In the Pale, and all that *móin a' bheatha* seeping through
The veins of a dangerous little bundle, a sickly child,
Who was the worth of two poets in two languages,
Who heard 'wings of parchment shake and bells weep'.

MARTIN ROCHFORD'S MEMORY

From his fingers I heard
The famine cries of children and eviction,
The sound of the bokety cart wheel
On The Green Road going down
To the sea for departure,
The sigh of the convicted felon
On the whim of a landlord's lie.

Hidden Ireland danced
Amongst the black-toothed fields
In Corkery's clouded countryside,
Where the whispering conversations
Spoke of great events in the spring-
Time birth of lambs and summer
Swish of hay saved in the rain.

He was our Woodstock
In the struggling 70's of historical
Millstones, our salvation in Bodyke
Or Feakle between The Beatles
And Bob Dylan, piping us into
A future where the past could be
Faced with the clarity of his note,
Steadfast as our heartbeat.

THE KNIFE SHARPENER OF MADRID

We know him by his work-bike and the shrill
Notes of a panpipe - a curlew winged with pellets,
The moan of a moorcock in the meadow-trap.

Once I brought him a blunt one and he fanbelted
A reflection of my soul, a blade for slicing airs.
He is the pied piper of acrimonious tongues,

Flash of steel at cash points, a stinging wind
That wears us down to size, the daily grind
Of blue-iced mornings. When he calls again

I will bring him a fistful of nibs for honing
In his likeness, a satchel of inert wits
To match those of my colleagues.

LOS BRIGADISTAS EN EL PALACIO DE DEPORTES 1997

for Tom Enthwistle

'Hermanos, Madrid con vuestro nombre se agrada y se ilumino'

Rafael Alberti

Who failed to feel the chill of their courage
On our spines that night, the clenched fist
Of a more peaceful age, the glint of bravery
In our medallionless eyes – Living idols this side
Of a fifty-year-old Civil War grave?

Those men and women come home to Spain
To proudly claim their Pasionaria invitation;
Walk unforgettable outlines of battlegrounds
Where comrades fell; gave their young lives
To manure the olive fields with freedom.

Who among us did not tremble when history
Spoke and legend real as flesh, in voice recalled
Galapagar and Morata cemetery outside the wall –
Where the dumped remains of the Jarama dead
Were finally brought in for honourable rest?

And who, if Irish failed to hear Wolfe Tone's plea
To 'abolish the memory of all past dissension';
Embrace the International names of those
Heroic examples of democracy whose presence
Stalked prosperity's indifferent streets,

Reduced noisy bars to silence, raised questions
In young minds about lost Republics,
The acceptable face of King Juan Carlos.
Those men and women of a more generous age
Who fought and died defending its citizens.

ALTRUISTIC VOICE

The void slowly fills with ordinary
Conversation about whether to buy
Small or large fruit bowls, a gooooal
Scored on the radio, snatches of laughter
Along indecently strollable streets
In late summer here, early fall there,
Where a woman on a mobile
From a plane on its way to oblivion,
Pleads "What can I do?" as her husband
Sees a tower explode and crumbles.

This page should be forever blank
As the colour of pain or Picasso's dove
Guiding us to an indomitable tree in winter
Snow, alive with dignified response,
Wind-prayer for these inadequate words.
But the need for language to express
Defies the emptiness, replenishes the space
With spoken or solemnly read messages,
Tender as the flame of a night-light –
A warm tear for the living and the dead.

THE LOST SCRAPBOOK OF '66
for my teacher Eric Lynch

1
The idea shaped by the Christmas gathering of uncles
And their political disputes over Collins or Dev,
The exact pole where O Donoghue was shot when taken
From my grandfather's house that night of triple murder.

The cards played on the question mark in the smoked air -
Why was one spared? The answer as I had heard it between
The pouring of whiskey and water: to plant the Black & Tan
Doubt in the ranks, sow the seed for future argument

And betrayal. My father, the younger peacemaker on the piano,
Recalled with humour the touch of bayonet on the stairs in '21,
A song from my mother She Moves Through the Fair,
Recitations of Bredon Hill and The Tinker's Son, a rebel ballad

From the rebel uncle, silent approval from the Mayor,
As we children hucklebucked the night to a close of half-
Crowned farewells under a sky of uncertain promise.

2
Lost to me now I renew the task our teacher set the class of '66 -
And the years have not diminished those maligned men and women
In the third Millennium, nor cleansed the memorabilia of history
As it happened for me: confessional secrets between the lines,

The aftermath of cannon fire from ruins where green uniforms
Appeared like heroes from other wars, to be incarcerated or shot,
Their Proclamation a centre-fold of what it was all about, the index
A list of those who lived to tell their versions of the insurrection.

3

In the factory of lies so much rebutted since that audacious week.
Unthinkable happenings as though it were Goya's Tres de Mayo
In Dublin, the defiant faces of the defeated herded between spit
    and insult
To be tried for treason against an Empire about to disintegrate.

All those yellowing cuttings and tinted postcards, a 30's map of Irish
Names and origins, divided testimonies to Civil War between Post Office
Comrades in the rubble dying for the right to wear the English plumes.
Interviews with Tom Clarke's cousins and vivid repulsion of scandalous

Executions. In them I felt the prison breeze that touched the noble face
On its last dawn, the white cloth fluttering, pinned close to the heart
For shaming the aim of those who would have honour smirched,
Courage denied, the phoenix transformed into swine.

4

How time rights wrong in the scrapbook of the mind,
Deciphers the palpable sneer at the shared fortune of initialled
Pennies, the impoverished legacies of buttons prised from uniforms
As presents for the aggrieved families of Heuston and Colbert,

A Daly heirloom in a Limerick museum, Connolly's tender lock of hair
In Kilmainham, the fight for Irish freedom in a glass case in Clonmel.
From such items was prosperity's bungalow built,
And out of the ridicule of signatories to the words of a letter

Dismissed amongst the buffoons, derided in its discoloured neglect
On the wall of a Parnell Square bar, a spirit that moved others
To repudiate the congealed blood of colonial rage, ignite the will
To remove the boot from the pleasure garden, restore it to their liking.

5

Their ghosts came back to haunt the border towns
Like cattle raids on barrack buildings, challenged Carson's
Post Easter threat, the treatyfied statelet for apartheid.
What followed to the present Ireland's nightmare:

To unravel the consequences of opposing sides, the propped
Regime of favours, an oppressed eye on the South.
My own eyes blinded with sadness in Mrs McDonnell's living room,
Her son a selfless corpse, another hero for reconciliation.

6

This twelve year old turned twenty five no Armalite fighter
Nor terrorist in the new political climate, so mythology carried me
On the back of an estuary gull to the Irish street in Madrid,
To Finnegans' near O'Donnell's tomb, among the inoffensive ballads

No longer sung in the Euro cauldron. But we who are scarred or care
For another beginning think international for the wish to come true
In some near future, when one of us might live to defy the odds
Before death is waked on the bed of want.

Yeats' echo for my lost artefacts:
"Too long a sacrifice/Can make a stone of the heart",
That the same salt water of the one shore might heal the shared wound
Before the century finds its arrogant stride and bitter spit fuel
The tepid stove to sudden crow-caw of bomb-blast quaking
The gunshot freeways of the grove.

7

A scrapbook for 2016:
Proclamation of life as a coupling, the green of the grass
The kiss of the rain, the eye to snare such beauty,
Bloodless heart dead thing, no thought without a brain.

Lives lived in the shadow of an eclipsed sun, excavated
In a hundred years to come, the threads of a puzzling sash,
The silent scream for a more forgiving religion.

That the living might hear the voice of a united island
Unlike so many before them, shun the bigot on the torched
Hillside, the venomous beat on the skin of the big drum,
The quagmired scribe at large with vindictive tongue

And see through blindfolds with firing-squad vision,
How to turn the obstinate key of mutual recognition
Into a fairer future for the other's suffering and survival.

8

My dead uncles never saw the answers to their questions
And my mother's people learned to keep tight counsel
With the post-Cromwellian blush of the convert, their true
Colours noted in the Ballingarry Famine Relief Scheme,

In a safe house for those on the run, a graveyard in Donaghmore,
Far from the family plot in St Mary's Cathedral.
Could I but have had some of my mother's composure,
Heed her last words of "not to worry about that Irish/English thing,

It will sort itself out in time" Yes, I promised, I will, as I turned
Away with my brothers to see the Shannon's spinal strength
Coursing through the pages of the scrapbooked towns and villages,
Between the banks of the living and the dead, along the majestic
Length of the Island, down to the sea and beyond…

RECALLING MOTHER

The endless road to recovery sparkles with strange magic –
A pillowed butterfly, the chirp of a lodged bird in the room.
On either side your presence shines through the openings.
A girl's delight on a street in Seville, discovering the smell
of oranges overhead or the sudden release of my arm
In Cordoba, like the interception of an old thought, my father
The son you walked beside, remembering strolls to the Spa
In Lisdoonvarna and other magnolia-scented, antique-lit,
Honeymoon couples going the extra mile to Gus O'Connor's
Or dancing in the Hydro.

There was so much else I wanted to show you on your visits
To Madrid – the preparation of bulls' meat after the Corrida
Might have appealed to that meticulous eye for the best piece
Left to hang, or trips to warmer islands other than solitary winter
Reading in the middle of storms; friends and acquaintances
Orphaned or estranged, their confessional hurt comforted
By tactful counsel, like Cura's young mothers who did not
Absent themselves from your composed farewell.

So much else to explain. The swallow path in Tiorabháin,
A tabernacle in the sea, why seed birds peck thistles differently.
But you did not wish for more as you lay there in your favourite
Blackberry dress and orchestrated the scene as planned: a choir,
A song, a homily, a poem, the gospel of St. John, Mo Ghrá Thú
From the graveside hill, soup for the traveller and intimate supper
In a local hotel, that singsong at a wedding before departure.
No further revelation could make the journey without you
More acceptable, or fill my eyes with the goodness
I have known despite this empty pain.

POSTERITY

The continuance of stone
talking in the memory
of those who remember
the metaphor

The scent of fledgling
evaporating in a matchbox
changing colour
on its way to dust

The terrified fawn
limping through rushes
away from the car
you were travelling in

The web's destruction
or the boot-crush
on the long march
across your path

These events are given
to one who will recall
in time you telling them
such trivia

Reborn in the story-
teller's art the stuff
of epic and legend
woven out of life

It is how we never
really disappear
always almost
oblivion

Wine and Hope

(1999)

POEM
for my brother Liam

Inside the poem
The faint tormented rumblings of the loft.
Thoughts and images of permanent dark,
Butterflies struggling towards spring.
Ignorance, some truth, fallibility,
Until finally a beginning to rid
The poem of what doesn't sing.

Inside the poem
The sea-shell echo of love
Keening in your ear, dreams of famine
Devouring the flesh of faces pure,
Eyes that scream explosion;
Gulls among fields of crow
Waiting for the storm to blow,
Caged birds spurning what binds them.

Inside the poem
Places where the mind delights –
Birth of river, bend of mill-road,
Black strand of washed up shark bone,
Lake, city, sierra, places nowhere,
Paths across invisible stone,
Depths within reach of the poem.

PRAYER FOR PEIG

The click of the free wheel the cause
Of my jumping to open the door on my
Beret-bearing aunt of basketed gifts.

All those rainsome half-day Thursdays
Of child-minding the boggling questions
About God and why I could not see him.

And always before bed the fussy hands
Washing me clean with suds and saintly
Metaphors until I slept with crossed

Arms and dreamt of being the priest
You wanted me to be. Over the years
We hammered the religious punchbag

Found acceptance, respect for the lay
Nun's heart, the celebrant in the poet.
Dear Peig, hear now the poem in my

Prayer, the part that whispers of grace
And heavenly leave-taking from a world
No longer of your ilk, old stock.

THREE PAINTING BY JOHN SHINNORS

1.

There is a family eating on the riverbank
And as families sometimes do, they could
Be eating each other, except for a young man
Who looks as though he just might run.

My brother in his sleep used to knock
That painting from our bedroom wall,
So I placed it in the attic but the nightmare
Went on, as in The Picnic.

2.

Into that blue-bone, pre-dawn cold the bent
Back of a cyclist twice his weight in pain,
Moves along a road black as bog oak.

The bicycle, unseen, carries him towards
A winter storm or a promise of summer
Glory in the mountains of France and Spain.

3.

The snail is a helicopter in the night.
A Spielberg fantasy. Never again to be crushed
By boot or eaten as a delicacy. But worshiped
As the future speed for our slow ways.
A new Messiah. God evolved.

IN THE SILENCE OF THE HUNT MUSEUM
for Patrick F. Doran and i.m. of John Hunt

And there at the welcoming watch
Apollo from Augsburg - Genius of the Arts,
Muse to lives dedicated to excellence,
Bearer of the world's trades and crafts.

Once inside, a triptych of bronze soundings:
Decorated bucket humming of spring rain,
Ceremonial ring of Yetholm shield,
Cauldron kindling the festive hillside.

He is astray in other places and times:
Sampling whiskey from Henry Delamain's
Spirit barrel, safekeeping the Antrim Cross
In a German cellar lit by the glow

Of Candelabra - a stag's head from Beleek;
About his waist a gold torc from Granta Fen
And in his pocket a silver hawk's bell
Engraved with the arms of James 1.

He is the murmuring of the beads
In the hand of the priest on the run,
Wet to the bone from the sleet of the Rock,
His penal pilgrimage rubbed smooth

For warmth, the bright days of his glory
In the clear note of the Cashel Bell,
His aftertaste in the Communion Cup of Mothall:
The monastic screams of his plundering

Still heard in the sword he swung at Durrow,
The echo of the spear's flight like wind
Blowing in off Gur. He is the arrow flint
In the flesh of the great bog deer,

A polished stone from that age -
Should you listen you will hear yourself
As dust trembling in encrusted urns,
Phantoms shifting in Lekythoi, laughter

Of drinkers in Tudor jugs, wounds
Healed in majolica and owl jars.
He is unity and effort, form and grace,
The patinated axehead's cry of release.

THE BURIAL OF A NUN

I had been classifying The Lives
Of the Saints when I was drawn
To the window by a plaintive bell,

A chorus of voices answering
The bishop's prayers; black habits
Indelible as ink against the frost.

I felt a privileged sense of shame,
Of not belonging but welcome,
An intruder afraid of being seen

At such an intimate gathering,
The old pang of venial sin.
Then the garden blossomed

With celestial singing, in praise
Of one who died for the words
I was cataloguing. I turned

To the books of my lost faith
And saw how I too had to find
My own library of truths.

Beyond the convent wall
The blasphemous noise
Of the city waited for me.

TO MARCUS IN THE COMING YEARS

Badh sealbh aoibhneasta an t-eolas
(Happiness comes with knowledge)

You may ask in time what the world
Was like when you were born
And I will say, among other things,
How I walked the Christmas streets
Home on air, whispering your name
And the name of your mother.

I will tell of America's cardboard poor,
The volatile rebirth of Russia,
Highland stirrings, Basque explosions,
Weeping waterfalls in Plitvice,
Death of rivers, zoo stuffed animals,
The chainsaw termiting of the forest,
The last of Europe's archaic colonist.

And as you search my eyes for answers,
Question the inadequacy of my replies,
I will show you, among other things, how
To flinch for the pain of the lame dog,
Reach for the high note of birds,
Embrace the best of two worlds.

SONG FOR SEÁN

Now is the moment for impervious water to break
And new life's push and gush towards light begin,
Though Goya's predawn winter witches beckon
The scythe of tomorrow's descent back to dark.
Pale with anticipation for you and your mother
I idle dilatory time eyeing headlines of the day.
What will be left to embrace out of such decay
When my hands bleed the print of your future?
But this is the prelude you should never forget:
Our first words and wishes of love and welcome,
To consider the best of two worlds your home
And see in both those festering wrongs put right
Round a unified table of tolerance more humane,
The reins of a fairer destiny grasped again.

HEINRICH BÖLL IN LIMERICK

Not a sinner on the street when you arrived.
A sharp reminder of curfew times again.
Then the churches emptied and you found
Yourself part of the miracle crowd.

In the bar where you lodged called The Green Door
I used to think of your visit when reading
The Lost Honour of Katrina Blume.
You among the great thirst quench

And placing of bets, the laughing well-fed faces,
Some of whom wished Germany had won.
How you must have mused on the indifference
Shown to that destruction when you noted down

In your Irish Diary the nothing much to observe,
Relearned the value of unlikely places,
The black bread of those earlier years,
Left accounts that cut to the bone.

CUT STONE: JIM KEMMY (1936-1997)

"Who owes a debt to this great man"

It was a 1960's comeback to "a 1950's time-warp"
For a surrogate father in his "numbed" twenties
"Forced out to a pagan world by hopeless unemployment",
Plagued with "relentless feeling of inadequacy";
Returned to a "wounded response in Limerick",
"Home to Garryowen, without glory".

This he wrote for bitter-free purpose:
To find the grain of cold indifferent stone;
Dismantle the ballast that anchored the poor
To criminal wage, kept their families accumulating;
Crushed whatever smacked of change, threatened
Cosy church or latter-day William Martin.

Larkinesque in mind and stature, Connolly
Without the gun, he chiselled away at intolerant
Walls of sieged mentalities, until he found
The opening, and with his bag of socialist tools
Organised a Union, chronicled what he saw,
Set the progress of a City in motion.

He was the fist in the arena of political clout
For the marginalized and the voiceless,
The Saturday morning ear for local complaint,
A one-salaried TD and Mayor, paver of lonely paths,
A modern Maurice Lenihan or John Ferrar,
Poet and small farmers' friend.

Above the sing-song chorus of that mirrored bar
I heard gentleness of shy greeting again; saw truth
Evaporating with a smile. I had followed him as far
As I could and in return he showed me how to chip
At what disdains, make our lives and where we come
From exemplary in the eyes of a bigger stage.

BLUES PIECE
for Sheila

In your dreams
You remember what can not
Be explained. Wake tired,

More troubled.
That little guilt, a misdeed,
Follows you around,
Niggling inside your head.

Were it not for habit
And the ability to forget,
Fear could kill.

You doubt the next breath,
Hide the panic,
Muffle the scream,
Know how to pretend.

But, Sheila, remember this:
We are all uneasy
In our skin.

LANGUAGE LESSON

I wanted to open their minds
To the word as I had heard it
On my way to them:

"The terrorists of....
Sorry, I'll read that again.
The territories of..."

Open their minds to the tricks
And subtleties, shifts of emphasis,
The sly diplomacy of sounds.

Unravel the grammar of ornament,
The meaning of space on a page;
Read between the lines that lead

Into and out of the human cage.
I wanted them to know the lie,
If possible truth, so that all else

Would sicken in the mouth:
Belfast crucifixion, legalised
Barbarity, kidnap victim found

Dead in the Basque country.
I wanted them to know the bullet
That bounces off the moon,

Explodes in a man's back
Going home, the key in the car
Bomb. To listen for each syllable

Like a bird-note of freedom,
Wind blowing through an empty
Classroom, something other
Than this language lesson.

THE LAST HOUSE IN CONNAUGHT

To the memory of Micho Russell who played the tune of the title for myself and
Knute Skinner one evening in O'Connor's pub, Doolin, County Clare, Ireland.

Any old country road will do to hear its version of the future.
In the closing time voices accustomed to the dark or delirious
Shadows with their coded messages for change – so close
They may as well be far out at sea along with the stubborn
Stone in the middle of a field or the thorny ditch like a stray
Cat's scratch guarding its little patch of the past.

Any old country road will tell you how it was, is and wants to be –
Free of the blighted verges of its hungry dead, the potted
Hellholes of neglect. Road alive in the full flight of summer
Dance, of passionate winter dawns. Road that leads to the last
Latch where you may hang your heavy coat up on the floor
And listen to sweet tunes for young ears played by old fingers.

Surely you have imagined such a house where even the egg
Timer had stopped, plates of brown bread heaven on earth;
Known such people whose very kindness had the natural
Air of being uniquely special – ancestral survivors
Of Cromwell's merciless sword, their caved-in cottages
Monumental wounds of famine, burnt offerings of drunken

Despair to loves who fled to America. Surely you have stumbled
Across this landscape in any old knocked-down town reclaimed
Anew; recognised the pain on its broken walls, along the outline
Of slums and corner stones, in the smell of pulverised dollars
Sent home with letters of polite lies, too sad for spending
On a glow of hope in the empty grate.

Such towns yearn for balance between the sound of milk churn
And discotheque, market mule and rush-hour traffic, a sudden
Flock of sheep in the clean haze of exhaust fumes, the hum
Of the fuchsia bush – cravings for the centre of the heart's
Search, before the spine of the forgotten country road
Blisters and cracks in your palm.

MY GREEN BAR

i.m. John Jordan

Here was your stage, your theatre of recovery.
A Royal elegance in old Madrid,
a whispering anonymity.

From here you dreamed in Irish and Latin
of Orson, Oxford, Michael and Hilton,
Grogan's ghosts about your table,
all in a flickering candle.

Stories, plays, Offaly, Dublin, Pamela and Gainor
waving white from the bull ring, the dawn
chill of a park bench in the Málaga rain,
Catalan poems of Pearce Hutchinson,
Patrick Kavanagh, Gerald Brennan,
La pobre Miss Katie in the hotel Jardín.

Here in the dark candlelit corner you played
at being a house plant in a green vase
that occasionally needed watering.

Everything green, so you said you seemed to fit.
From here you imagined a glorious
curtain call, a sudden death.

A DRY WELL IN SALAMANCA

In the bare and simple centre
The webbed scholarship
Of centuries on its sides.
The echoless laughter of newly
Arrived Irish Seminarians.
Where the light shines through
A touch of the glory past
On a lick of fern.

This sealed off source
Of learning, a locked inkwell
(as though somebody might fall in)
where the gargoyle's disdain
is frozen in stone and no wish
made or vellum touched by quill.

THE CORNER STONE
for Puy

Chipped by centuries of safe homecoming
Along tight streets where no lamp shone,

That polished granite-resting place
Steadfast, tenacious, almost forgotten.

The cart wheel worn to a mouldering blade,
Pulverised among the weeds in a backyard,

Old halos of thunder and spark
Flaked by much more than mere stone.

A beginning, like the first book
In a library for young minds,

Guiding them out of a corner
Towards the open spaces of their lives.

MADRID THROUGH THE EYES OF A STRANGER
For Ita Fitzgibbon

Crossing the French border by bus
Was like passing through a doorway
Into a warm barn. Finally, wearily,
Happily in Spain among the bar crowds
And tapas, The Third Man music
From the slot machine.

Then south into a centre of bulls
And late summer lust, football, festivals,
Mus and park bowls, fountains frozen
In a winter frost, where "the sea is in
A glass of gin", the bonamhs wear bowler hats,
"Englis Spoken" near shops that sell
Caramelos Paco and the largest corsets,
Where the trumpet player balances a goat
On a stool, the rug seller shoulders
The sun, the dancer moves like a harlequin
To the churning of the tune,
Where "Hemingway never drank here".

This city of newly arrived unloved,
With eyes like eager sailors,
Missing the beat, but finding it,
Among the bodega silence
Of Goya's old failures.

Song of the Empty Cage

(1997)

SONG OF THE EMPTY CAGE
excerpts: **Part One**

Freedom is my song
Song of the caged bird
Sorrow my absence.

When sad I am empty
But when free I sing
Knowing what binds me.

> *In the days of Fionn*
> *And the Fianna they loved*
> *The hills not prisons.*

> *Blackbird language*
> *Is what they knew*
> *Not the crudity of sirens.*

> (from Binn Sin, A Luin Doire An Chairn)

Lover I have been
In the air and in those soft
Pockets of sungrass.

Such songs afterwards
In the warm pools
I...hear.

> *Welcome to the bird who sweetens*
> *The branch, laurel of loveliness*
> *Who makes the bushes beam.*

> *Long and wearisome is my life*
> *When I don't see her coming*
> *As the grass turns green.*

> (from Fáilte Don Éan: Seamus Dall Mac Cuarta)

I have sat in the belfry
Of Glenstal Abbey
Listening to voices

Echoing in Irish
The story of a country
Once named after me.

Sweet music,
Not bad at all.
Pity more don't follow

The free song of the bird
And not be blasting us
Out of the sky.

> *I don't sing for the song*
> *Nor for the good voice I possess,*
> *I sing because the guitar*
>
> *Has meaning and reason,*
> *Has heart of land*
> *And wings of little doves.*
>
> *(from Manifesto: Victor Jara)*

Igmoramuses
Whose betters became
Secret and quiet

When mentioning my name.
Drew in their breaths
Should the vision become known.

> *Beauty born from the Kings*
> *Of Ulster, careful,*
> *Hold your tongue.*
>
> *That treasured little bird*
> *Who made the boughtips laugh,*
> *Don't mourn: its but lime-dumb.*
>
> *(from An Lon Dubh Báite: Seamus Dall Mac Cuarta)*

Windswept round corners,
Brokenwinged and hungry,
I have been kicked

The full length of alleyways
Only to be rescued
By my traditional enemy.

I saw a cat stalk a bird,
Stealth in each step,
Sure of its approach;

But at the hour of the kill
The bird rose –
Such is how age comes.

From *Dánta 1939-1979: Máirtin Ó Direáin)*

Extraordinary the hands
That befriend me.
Mostly those of prisoners,

The mad and the lonely.
For them I sing
Heavenly symphonies.

Because within the sad garland
Of the link, of the constant
Taste of jailer and firing squad,

About to be taken out, tall
Happy, free, I am. Tall, happy
Free, free, only for love.

(from *Cancionero y Romancero de Ausencias:*
Miguel Hernandez)

To have crossed that stream,
Rounded its bend,
Was to have flown between

Peig's view of heaven
From a graveyard
In Dun Chaoin.

When I die bury me
With my guitar beneath the sand.
When I die, between the oranges

And the mint. When I die
Bury me if you wish
In a weather-vane. When I die.

(from Momento: Federico Garcia Lorca)

Dead I will sing
In the belly of the worm's
Revenge. Otherwise

Dumb. Grounded
My brothers will fill the air
With funeral notes.

excerpts: **Part Two**

It was a morning of black
Scattering road, of funeral
Gathering above the oaks

When I set out in search
Of new mythologies, a cure
For the hurt in my bones.

In solitude she lives,
And in solitude she has
Now built her nest,

And in solitude her
Lover alone guides, also
In solitude love hurts.

(from Cantico Espiritual.
Canciones Entra El Alma y El Esposo: San Juan de la Cruz)

What I missed most was
The smell of green after rain,
The drip of sunlit hedge

The waterlogged warmth
Of fields, sea breeze
And a grove full of friends.

Bliss for the small birds
Who rise so high and quaver
On the one branch together.

Not like me and my eternal
Love who must rise everyday
So far from each other.

(from Nach Aobhinn Do Na hEiníní)

I grew thin. I longed
For another season, a little
Sun to give my eyes some feasting.

Rivers lay stagnant
In my veins and in my dreams
There were no carnivals.

A dove between the wires, still.
Without flight, light or north.
Or making air: only thedarkness

And the gentle cooing of the night.
Tell me, divine one, why only
In solitude he comes.

(from Retracciones: Fanny Rubio)

High upon Txindoki,
Sacred mountain of Basques,
I saw between the clouds

What Euskadi is:
Heavenly words of wind
And air spoken by mortals.

Such beauty I have seen before,
Rained on by the blood of those
Who believe it worth fighting for.

Should there be peace
Will we break down and weep
For the withered flower?

In the North Sea, in the South Sea,
Nothing like water, nobody like you.
In the brown earth, in the blue sky,

Nothing like the air, nobody like you.
In the dark shade, in the clear light,
Nothing like the fire, nobody like you.

(from Madrigal: David Cherican)

Among the Roman ruins
Of Tiermes a knife wind
Cuts through the once

Great halls of Soria's
Conquerors, mocking all
Such earthly powers.

Beekeeper is my love
And in his hive
Bees of gold come and go.

Of your hive
Beekeeper of the soul
I behive.

(from Canciónes Del Alto Duero: Antonio Machado)

There the sound of water
Whispering to water, shade
Concealing Arab and Moor.

Light, stone, bird, flower,
Blending in a poem
That is Alhambra.

Inside my guitar there is an old air,
Dry and sonorous, permanent, motionless,
Like a faithful nutrition, like smoke:

An element of rest, a vivid oil:
A hardy bird who minds my head:
An angel invariably alive in my back.

(from Sabor: Pablo Neruda)

I fly back to where I must leave.
Look on the changed faces
Of friends looking at me.

I hope they see the love in my eyes.
That part which is still
Part of their lives.

The Angling Cot

(1991)

RAINBOW ROAD
for Nora McNamara

Among sharp fragments
Of dangerous delta glass,
Milk streams turned a grey complexion,
Rush hour dust shifted
From footpath into gutter
Into any crack.
Seven-year-old tears fell on pale stone,
Embarrassment conceived a childish crime
Out of such an innocent act.
Another shade of confusion
Crept across the wet
Illuminated road home.

Older, cuter, yet seemingly
Disinterested in adult theory,
Personal preoccupation slackened:
A leather sandal on a rubber sole,
A stocking below an ankle –
As the lazy beat of greasy rain
Built its own ice rink
And like ink blobs on white paper
Paraffin oil crudely kissed
The original skin of cloud water.
More than seven colours
Fashioned the pattern of Rainbow Road.

REMEMBERING MR TOPPIN

Out of the mouths of crows he swooped,
A red faced wing commander,
Low flying over the big house,
His landlord's eye upon us.

In him we felt the crack
Of his Anglo-Irish whip whenever
He rode to hounds or snapped
In his once great laundry rooms.

He was a world of ponies and traps,
Of dance bands on moonlit lawns,
Keeper of the sweetest apples,
A hide-away among the gardens.

Now only elm and sycamore
Stand like sentries with nothing
to guard, as factories edge
To where the front door was.

SCARECROW

I have heard the egg crack
In a wren's nest. The wind snap
At the thistle tip of every sting.
Once there were two spiders

On a quilt of toasted leaves,
Each with its own blueprint
For its own invisible web.
One hunter I knew could kill

A fox before his gun dog sniffed
The scent. I have seen a river
Doll tug free from those stones
Born on river beds and challenge

The battering course of another
Journey. I have cheered the walk
And tumble of a foal in her
Mother's blood, cursed those boots

That crushed the ripe stalks
Of my pride. I am a scarecrow
Nailed to old wood, eaten
By worms, paralysed by rust.

POUND DEVALUED IN WHITE HOUSE
(title by Séamus Ó Cinnéide)

It was suggested to the proprietor
That he remove a photograph of Ezra Pound
Before Robert Graves
And his entourage of chosen literati
Entered Gleeson's old world White House
In the thrice sieged city
Of Limerick.

The erudite barman
Understanding the critical
Implication of such a request
Promptly placed the out-of-favour Pound
Behind a snap shot of local poet
Gerard Ryan.

There he remained
While the eminent Don
Sat recalling the times
When his father drank whiskey
From the same barrel and heated his rump
By the same fireside.

When the hour came round to leave
Mr. Graves autographed
A photograph of himself
For Mr. Gleeson.

Today it hangs beside Mr. Pound
And still not a word between them.

EMMET DALTON

You did the Irish thing
By fighting for England in defence
Of smaller nations,

Returning from the Somme
With professional war experience
To join your own countrymen

In the slaughter of each other.
Free Stater, Pro Treatyite,
Body guard to Michael Collins,

You helped your side to win,
Beating De Valera's republicans
Into submission.

Major General at twenty-three,
Resigning over the question
Of Military Courts,

Member of the first Seanad,
Seller of whiskey,
Founding visionary of Ardmore

Film studios,
Tireless worker for a country
That didn't know how

To bury you properly,
Whose Government abstained
From your funeral

Because you happened to be
On the wrong side
Over fifty years ago.

A VISION OF DE VALERA FROM A BUS IN BRUREE

It was as though he cloaked
The land again and all past events
Seemed to melt with a sudden burst of sun.
From where I sat high above the Maigue
History was less than truth
And fact a thing of plastic consumed
By the smallest flame.

What matter then that he tried
To shape a country with his own hands,
Or once transformed villages
Into Greek arenas when playing
Homer at political rallies.

In the darkness of his last years
Perhaps this is what he wanted:

An old man and a boy
Walking by the river of his childhood,
The sun tossing fish into the sky,
Green fields spread out like Paxton's
Chatsworth, a warm eternal peace
In Bruree where people
Could sit and drink Guinness,
Not always at ten to three.

SOUTHERN COMFORT

In '69 it was different.
Something had to be done.
So we turned up our television sets
And replaced the game of 45
With talk of war.
But it never happened
At least not in the South.
So we grew careless
With the daily atrocities
And took to the cards again.

Then the bombs went off
In Dublin, Galway, Limerick
And Killarney,
So we beat our knuckles
On counters of self pity
And swore to 'join the boys'.
We were angrily suspicious
And talked about reprisals.
When the damage and the dead
Were known we sat around
The pulpit and shaped
Our prayers like bullets.

Now we refer to the killing
As 'the troubles'.
We are thankful to God
For the Sunday morning chat,
The quiet pathway home from the pub.
We look forward to the annual
Dinner dance, are stirred
By the occasional public debate.

But we know what it means
To be a majority.
We know how to tip our caps
At our confessors
Who would forgive us anything.

POULO, GALICIA
for Susana Montero

Close to the northern lights
Of forgotten Portuguese vilelas,
I was home again among low rock walls,
The smell of gorse and heather,
Orujo – my illicit drop of poitin.

And but for the vine and the sun
Lit lemon, picked for the first time,
I could have been watching a woman
With a hand scythe knee deep
In the lush grass of a strange field in Clare,

Or men from West Kerry with eyes
Sweetened by wind, wine and air.
So familiar was this longing in lives
Lived tight as laneways, rooted to priest
And myth, insular, proud as Islanders.

KATE O'BRIEN IN AVILA

for Jaime Ramos

Here was the Spain she loved most.
The white light of her heart's content.
Among market faces rooted
In a Limerick childhood,
The Encarnación her Laurel Hill.

High within the walled embrace
Of Teresa's Castile.
Its cathedral silence
Touching her like fingertips
In a candlelight intimacy of friends.

WAITING
for Fran

I am painting the walls
With my eyes. bluebells, dog violet,
Gorse and heather, barnowls,
Puffins and Bewick swans.
Where a cobweb hangs –
Velazquez's faces of The Drinkers.

I am a small boy again.
My father is doing business in the bars.
Through the windows he looks
Like a gangster, a kidnapper
Making deals with a childless couple.
I will grow up to be a pint-pulling farmer,
Wear rubber boots and smell of dung.

Once I waited two hours in the rain
And thought of everything under the sun.
I was a hero returned from no war,
A lover of Chinese women,
The world's first immortal,
I was Godot.

Now I am waiting
As the bell waits to be rung,
As the door waits to open.

WORDS FOR SAMUEL BECKETT

I read on.
Understanding less.
Yet I could not leave you.
Each word brought
Me to the next.

Then days of brooding.
Of difficulty.
Until little by little
I saw the word complete.
Felt as my own heartbeat.

I read on.
The same problem.
But always the word
Keeping me in touch.

Out of such ignorance
I learned much.

THUNDER

Whenever I hear thunder
I think of Joyce,
Hiding under the big bed
Of his father's Dublin house,
Or forsaking the next drink
In the bars of Paris and Zurich,
To run for dear life
Into Nora's arms.

I think of Fionn before
And Fionn again,
And how all the rivering
Waters run,
Leafy as the Liffey
In the hearts of Molly and Bloom,
The dark mutinous Shannon
Calling me home,
The dead reawakening
Like love outside the room.

And I think of his words
Outweathering the storm,
Still thundering from under
The big wide bed of his world.

IN MEMORY OF MY FATHER

Windblown

All that week the wind and the sound
Of mowing and the silent raking in
Before drizzle turned to rain
And night brought a different scene

To a sick room blessed with the scent
Of green, of incense for the recurring
Apparition; perfume for the most
Beautiful child he had ever seen.

All those last days, my father looked
Out the window and saw himself again,
Windblown as a boy fielding a high
Ball in the big freshly cut world of June,
Unknowingly touched by the grass
That moved so quickly.

Breath

When he closed his hand
Round mine and his last sound,
Soft as bird-breath,
Filled the whole room

I saw how death had made
Those hands more beautiful,
Took their weight of crates
And gave them back a soul

As though he still played
Some rhapsody in blue
And we were together again
On the magical road to Doolin.

GOOD THINGS
for Joe Malone

I am consoled by the love of things.
Things quiet and gentle for the eye
To rest on. For thought to equal
Itself out again. Things ordinary
And simple. Like the casual sweep
Of a brush or the feel of cloth
Between finger and thumb.
Things momentary and accidental.
The way a sleeping wasp might turn
In a hollow knot of wood. Good
Things found on street and floor:
Acorn, feather, colourful string.
Things that get lost in the pile up
Of things huge and bewildering.

EMPTYNEST

In the silence of her house
My mother sits and remembers
The energy that once was.

She thinks of Christmases past
And the noisy unwrapping of hearts,
The small hours of musical evenings

And hears again the pandemonium
Of snap-apple nights when we as children
Jumped for those impossible bites

Or raced round the room
In search of the silver sixpence
That was my father's eye.

Such energy she doubts existed
Now that the piano's shut tight
As a coffin lid, the room
Where she sits full of silence.

TREATY OF LIMERICK
for Steve Keogh

It is winter in Clare
And the great rock empties
Itself into the sea. I am of flood
And silt on the ocean wave,
Bright spray salmoning a cliff path.

All that I am about me.
Windblown inland, storied across
Ground, where time long gone
Still beats beside the lake,
On hilltop cairn and gallery grave,
Among the singing bronze,
In every stone blessed by Patrick.

All that I am begun round
The bare marsh of Raven the Traveller –
Viking, Gael, English, Norman,
Each strand woven on my tongue –
Laxaweir, Rath, Bell and Tholsel,
The city and its fields my song.

Here in this cauldroned place
With its back to the river, I am
What life is: from a floating corpse
To a couples' kiss on the lemonade
Lips of summer, a mid-day scream
Of pigs at the slaughter, a gentle
Strumming of guitar, churches,
Banks, butcher shops, sickly
Eyes and poor. All that I am
Grown from here.

City of poets, painters, stone
Cutters' messages in the walls,
Of blistering railway tracks
And girls blossoming like lilac,
Of great plans buried in the bars.
Where madness walks with sanity
Along the avenues and all
Is the beginning of my vocabulary.

City of no centre still warm to my
touch. Its pulse a beat in my head.
The one prismatic language.

THE BALCONY
for Pamela O'Malley de Crist

So many false starts.
The out-of-step confusion
Of days lost when I could not
Unlock the panic, temper
The rough beat in my veins.

Then a different view.
Another beginning from where
I felt again the naked wrist of time
In the sound of shutters closing,
Learned what had to be done

From the brick by brick growth
Of a building, untangled
Before my eyes the spitfire
Movements of swallows,
Their slippery language

A word nest on my tongue.
All this realised from
The cool gift of your balcony.
To make with whatever
I put my finger on.

Boundaries

(1974)

CONTACT
for Sabina

We shall return again to welcome
the stiff wind in from the Lough,
count the offbeat waters break
on firm shore and frontal reed,
shame any attempt of a dull day
in June to model our faces
with the blush of a summer put off.

We defined presence as you shared
a cold sensation with my colder touch.

Grading unfamiliar ground carefully
towards a boastful view of the Lough,
I held back a thorn branch to allow
you pass, unscratched through the gap.
Side by side our bodies sloped
down this noble mass of land -
important moments were upheld
as the swan came out from the rush.

Stepping higher up the hillock
the breeze caressed our gaining
and hand-leading you to the top
eyes located the occasion of anything:
the white cabin near the shore,
a thousand starlings working hard
beaks into the gut of inland worms,
cows trodding past the opening
to drink the evening's fill, a wading
bird flapping amongst the watercress.

I shall preserve touch with simple things.

Slowly probing across the summit,
old stone like hurtful teeth bulged
through tender grass, prominently
producing childhood fears that existed
beneath the step of my prying feet –

O ancient lore of Irish mythology
you became a truth that danced
from uninteresting schoolbooks
to the hillock where I stand.

Grazing stone slabs that once screened
some being of extraordinary size,
I walked the ring fort round again.
Contact was assured despite
the generations who divorced
fact from myth. I was glad
to have found these monuments –

forever to feel at home
with unfamiliar things,
the self-evident holds
too many uncertainties.

Later we met and joined
our separate tales into one.

SEQUENCE OF SEVEN OMENS
for Jim Burke

1.
A buried sheep skull
omitted from local
veterinary columns,
hollowed out
by the habitual rambler,
dismissed as a worthless find –
fractions of unearthed white bone
crackle and scatter to adjust
in each disunited den,
broken parts settle down
removed from personal
handling.

2.
Ireland

Sunset reclined
across green remoteness,
deliberating for hours
beneath the illusory level,
she neglected her duty
and the half-light
wandered into dark.

3.
Boundaries of briar ditch and wild bush
calculate each limit of the ambling step.
Useful impediments blend perfectly
with feather and hide. Things brought,
things left are employed to serve –
the brown bean tin protects its tiny
occupants from the winter-dripping hedge.
Members are registered since creation,
cruel intruders have no connection.

4.
At the far end of Barry's field
Piled brambles concealed the opening.
Old Patsy stood beside the enclosure
Ponderously fingering a prickly thorn.
When he finished nursing the wet butt
His labouring hands set to work.
Layers of dead wood tossed the ditch,
Heavy anchor stones were placed to the side.
The trench field lost its concealment.

Dragging a brown sack through the clearing
Both eyes tracked a scattering of crows.
The chaffinch sounded acres away.
When the grass-trail reached the edge
He laid the bulky sack on the bank,
Tied the gripped cloth with briquette wire,
Held the bundle in his arms –
"She yelped as she sank to the bottom".

5.
Scorched stones still in their circle,
a begging basket of unwanted clothes,
basins reefed and buckets for the tin-smith,
a warped cart-wheel in need of repair,
broken cider bottles inside the ditch –
blood and holy Jesus
yo'll sleap undor de timbers tonit.

I hear their little differences
By the side of the road.
They are a civilization
of their own.

6.
ON CHRIST'S SADDLE
(Sceilg Mhichíl)

Mystical forces of monastic life
defend those tiring steps of age.
Great beehive huts, stone cross and grave
enshrine the presence of warrior and monk.
Solid rock steeped in wet solitude,
sanctuary for gannet and puffin,
residence for the lighthouse man.
Two lonely bulks of interest
Jutting awkwardly aloof
Nine miles from Valentia.

7.
UNDER THE UNCERTAIN PRESENCE

Under the uncertain presence
of some watery sun,
grey dominance weakened
isolated evenings
into noticing
the inflamed rust
from a poisoned stream.

Raising a wet crane
near the feet,
sounds of buckshot
buried him in air –
you cracked
the stranger's gun
with imaginary anger.

Then the greyness
broke its grip
to honour
the watery sun.